Through Sorrow Into

Through Sorrow Into

BY
Hugh M. Salisbury

BETHANY FELLOWSHIP, INC.
Minneapolis, Minnesota

Copyright © 1978
Bethany Fellowship, Inc.
All rights reserved

Published by Bethany
Fellowship, Inc.
6820 Auto Club Road
Minneapolis, Minnesota 55438

Printed in the
United States of America

**Library of Congress Cataloging
in Publication Data**

Salisbury, Hugh M
    Through sorrow into joy.
    1. Consolation. I. Title.
BV49052.S22   248'.86   77-13329
ISBN 0-87123-559-5

Hugh Salisbury

was born in North Dakota in November of 1929. He attended Central Washington College of Education. He married Miss Winifred Eells in the fall of 1953, and then continued his education. He spent 1953-55 at Simpson Bible College (then in Seattle), and took a B.A. degree in Education from Seattle Pacific University. He then earned his Master's degree in Religious Education and Counseling at Pepperdine University at Los Angeles. He was listed in "Who's Who in American Colleges and Universities" in 1957. He was also privileged to study at L'Abri Fellowship under Francis Schaeffer.

When his education was complete he spent fifteen years as Director of Christian Education and Youth in various churches. He has also been both a college and public school teacher for thirteen years. He is presently professor of Bible at Multnomah School of the Bible in Portland, Oregon, and makes his home in Portland with his wife and daughter, Janna.

Foreword

This is a beautiful day here in Island Lake Bible Camp in the Pacific Northwest. I am sitting by the fireside looking over the lake and finishing this manuscript.

This is the camp where my son found so much fun and help in his Christian life.

The book you are reading came out of our experience of the sudden death of our teen-aged boy. On January 6, 1970, Mark was walking 12 feet off the road when a car, traveling at a high rate of speed in a 30-mile zone, left the road and killed him instantly.

We were face to face

with the great enemy, Death.

We were unprepared for death. We have been Christians for many years, had family devotions in our home, but were not ready for the big test of death.

Our families and friends came to our aid immediately by being with us and praying for us. My brothers, Bob and Roger, came to our home as soon as they heard about Mark, and were a great help to me personally. Bob and his wife stayed with us for several days, giving us real strength through their physical presence. My wife was greatly comforted by her sister, Florence, who in her quiet way and in her willingness to listen was a tower of spiritual strength. Her parents and her brother, Merritt, were also present as a source of strength during difficult days.

I would like to express my sincere gratitude to our pastor, Rev. C. Wright Norton, who helped us move from sorrow to joy and to all of our dear family and friends who helped us during those days.

I would also like to express my thanks and acknowledge my indebtedness to the people who have helped to make this book a reality. First, my very close friend, Bill Clarke, for all his help and encouragement during those days, and now, with the manuscript. I would like to thank Mr. Larry Peabody for his first reading of the manuscript and for his special help in the early days of its preparation. A special thanks to two friends, Dr. David V. Myton and Dr. Samuel E. Sherrill, who worked long

and hard on this manuscript.

My sincere thanks to my dear wife, Freddee, who has been a great source of strength through all of these experiences, plus her faithful work in typing, retyping and editing the manuscript. Many thanks to my daughter, Janna, who was a source of power to us because of her childlike faith in the purpose of God.

As we were going through this experience, we turned to the Bible and there found the real hope and comfort that only God gives, and were "...turned from sorrow into joy" (Esther 9:22). The purpose of this book is comfort to those who have experienced death in the family.

Hugh Salisbury
Father of Mark Salisbury

Contents

I.	Who is calling?	13
II.	Why did it happen?	17
III.	What if?	23
IV.	Where should we turn?	27
V.	Why do people keep saying lost?	31
VI.	Where is he?	35
VII.	Will he live again?	39
VIII.	What will he be like	43
IX.	Where will we be?	49
X.	Can we go on?	55
XI.	How can we fill the void?	61
XII.	What will the future be?	67
XIII.	What has been gained?	73

I

Who is calling?

This was just another Monday—getting up early, and the children, Mark, age 12, and Janna, age 10, going off to school. That night my son and I went down to an outdoor basketball court to play ball and returned home for some good cookies my wife had baked.

Tuesday was a different day. We were up early as usual, for it was another school day, and a day of work for all of us. Breakfast is a time of family devotions for our family, and this particular morning our son read the Bible portion and led in prayer. Off to school went our two children. Our son came home for late lunch with his mother, then went out to deliver his papers for the day.

In the next hour our whole lives changed forever— never to be the same until the Lord returns with His saints.

Our son was 12 feet off the road when the car came speeding over the speed limit, ran off the road and hit and killed him instantly. Our lives were different from that moment on. We have never been the same.

Many, many questions came to our minds because we were faced with the greatest enemy of all, Death.

We were unprepared for physical death. We have been Christians for years, had family devotions in our home, but were not ready for the big test of death.

People gave us books, and some were a little help while others just made us feel worse.

Out of this experience come these questions, questions that I know you have asked a hundred times. This book contains a portion of our questions and the answers we received from the Word of God and the work of the Holy Spirit.

II

Why did it happen?

This is the very first question which came into our minds as we were together in the living room that afternoon. Why did it happen? Oh, why!

Was it because of something wrong that we had done, or because of sin in our lives that God was doing this thing? Or was it because our loved one had sinned and so was taken to heaven? Was God punishing us for something? Was it because we were not listening to God or were not teachable that God did this?

"Was this some form of punishment from God?" is always a question that tries to enter the hearts of believers. It is true that the Lord does correct His children. "Let God train you, for he is doing what any loving father does for his children. Whoever heard of a son who was never corrected?" (Heb. 12:7). We may have to harvest the fruit of mistakes and sin, or bear the consequences of what others have done. But the sin of the whole world was paid for by Jesus Christ on the cross of Calvary. If God were to punish you and me for our sins, it would mean that the Cross was incomplete, that the sacrifice was not enough. If this were true, life would be too short to pay for all of our sins.

Why then the great sufferings of saints like Paul, Peter and the happy lives of so many unbelievers? God is not punishing us—this was all taken care of on the Cross. Did God do this? "No," came back the answer. "God did not do this, but God did allow this to happen." Paul, writing in the book of Romans, said, " . . . prove what the will of God is, that which is good and acceptable and perfect." So God does have that which is acceptable but not perfect. We live in a fallen world with fallen people—that is, people who are in open rebellion against God—and this comes because of man's space-time-historic fall as given to us in Genesis. Because of this fall man is alienated from God, self, other men and from nature itself. Jesus said, "The rain falls on the righteous as well as the unrighteous," by this saying that all of us are a part of this world and therefore receive the good along with the bad. The world is full of both good and evil.

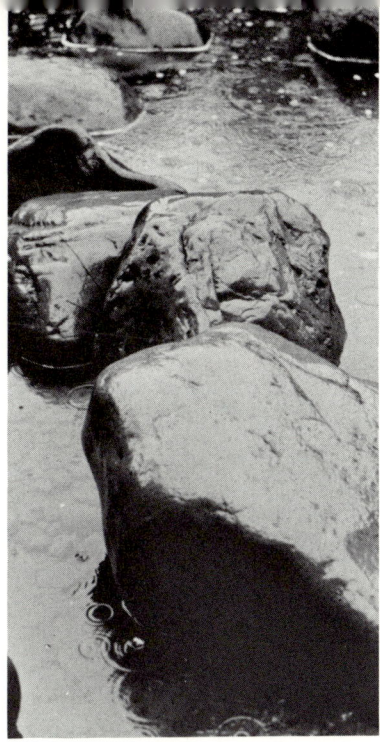

Even though we asked, "Why did it happen?" we were really only asking "Why at this time?" because we knew the meaning of Romans 5:12: "Therefore, just as through one man sin entered into the world, and death through sin, and so death spread to all men, because of sin."

We knew that our loved one was going to die a physical death, as we all will if Jesus doesn't come back first. Still we asked, "Couldn't this have been later?" Death is always too early. But we were looking at this with only our limited perspective, or to say it another way, from a point of limited knowledge. We know very little about the total of life, but God has all knowledge.

One of the cards which was sent to us said, "God is too wise to make a mistake and too loving to be cruel." This is "true-truth," because God is really there and He really loves. We cannot see all that goes on in the universe, but we can know from the book of Job that God really cares. Job, in his deep sufferings, did not know what was going on in heaven, but he believed God, for he knew who God really was. Based on the righteous character of God there will be justice, but when Jesus Christ comes back there shall be **absolute** justice in this universe.

Why did it happen? I honestly do not know, because of my limited knowledge, but more important is the fact that I know that my loved one is safe and happy with God. We do not have all the answers to this question, but we believe that God is really there and that He is personal and infinite. John tells us in his book that God has prepared a place for all believers and that we shall all be together some day. The future looks great. For as Christians our greatest days are ahead of us.

These thoughts were touchingly and concisely stated in a poem of consolation written for us by our friend, Sarah Jepson:

"Should the thing made say to the one who made it, why have you made me like this?"
(Rom. 9:20)

But why, O God, so young should he
Be called today to live with Thee?

One full of life, of boyish fun
And Lord, he was our only son.

Why grief for us who love Your name
And share the reason why You came,

Who long that families be complete
And worship daily at Your feet?

Why, when his life, You early claimed
And as a lad he has proclaimed

That Christ was his, Why this one?
Again, O God, our only son.

With fists clenched tight, and hearts that swell
We try to see—God does things well.

He gave this son to bless our home
But now desires him at His throne . . .

Where angel choirs, some his age,
Combined to set the celestial state

To welcome Mark to Heaven's shore.
(A resident there dies no more!)

Oh, can it be that God above
Has looked on us with tenderest love?

That He who spared not His own Son
Has asked for ours—and his "well done"?

If so, then, God, just let us be
Examples of those who are trusting Thee.

A family of three who know Christ lives
And when He takes, He also gives—

Glorious promises, hope to spare
Peace in heartbreak, sustenance through prayer.

Joy in tears, new love of friends
Everlasting LIFE which never ends.

What if?

Our son was always a careful boy, so we didn't really worry about him while he was out delivering his papers. On his first paper route he always stopped for prayer at a certain point just to thank God for His blessings.

These two words "what if" were among our first thoughts just after our Mark had been physically killed by a car. **What if** he had been in school? **What if** he had stayed home a little longer for lunch? **What if** he would have been more than 12 feet off the road? **What if** the youth in the car had not been driving so fast? **What if** we hadn't moved to this house? **What if** he hadn't had a paper route? What if . . . ? We could go on indefinitely asking similar questions because it is a natural response to the physical death of a loved one.

The answer to all "what if" questions is this: God is too wise to make a mistake and too loving to be cruel.

This assures my wife and me, persons with broken hearts, that God knew what He was doing. God had determined to take our son at this time to His home; the way He took him is irrelevant. This means that I trust that God knows the beginning from the ending, and that His highest purposes will be worked out, either in this life or in the life after. God knows best because He had all the knowledge we lack.

He knows all things—God is all-wise—He cannot make a mistake and still be God. The truth is that God does not make mistakes, and He has purpose and order in all that He does. We do not understand God's way, but we are to trust God that He knows what He is doing.

God is too loving to be cruel. God loves us—yes, He does. God cares—yes, He does. How do I know that God loves us? Because the Bible tells me so.

God gave His Son because He loves us, so that no matter what has happened, God really loves you and me.

"For I am convinced that nothing can ever separate us from his love. Death can't, and life can't. The angels won't, and all the powers of hell itself cannot keep God's love away. Our fears for today, our worries about tomorrow, or where we are—high above the sky, or in the deepest ocean—nothing will ever be able to separate us from the love of God demonstrated by our Lord Jesus Christ when he died for us" (Rom. 8:38, 39).

"For who among us can know the mind of the Lord?" (Rom. 11:34).

IV

Where should we turn?

One minute I was at a committee meeting talking about the Greater Seattle Sunday School Convention and the next moment I was in our front yard face to face with a state trooper telling me that our boy had been hit by a car. He was dead. We drove down to the morgue to see—and it was our son who was physically dead. Our question: "Where should we turn?"

We called our families, who came immediately and were the greatest help and support that one could ever ask for at a time like this. Our pastor came and was such a great help and encouragement along with many, many Christian friends who gave us real support during the first few days and weeks.

During those moments, though, we had called upon God, and He gave us something that only He can give: "peace—perfect peace."

Peace—perfect peace. Is that possible for God's people during their days of sorrow and grief? Yes, we found it so, because God is the giver of perfect peace. "I have told you all this so that you will have peace of heart and mind. Here on earth you will have many trials and sorrows but cheer up, for I have overcome the world" (John 16:33).

Don't worry about anything; instead, pray about everything; tell God your needs and don't forget to thank Him for His answers.

God, through the power of the Holy Spirit, can and will fill the heart full of peace. Only God gives peace of heart, the emotional tranquillity assuring us all is well. We received peace of mind from the Scriptures by knowing where our loved one is and that we shall all be together someday. "Don't worry about anything; instead, pray about everything; tell God your needs and don't forget to thank him for his answers. If you do this you will experience God's peace, which is far more wonderful than the human mind can understand. His peace will keep your thoughts and your heart quiet and at rest as you trust in Christ Jesus" (Phil. 4:7). His peace is like a policeman before the White House, keeping out all intruders who would harm the President. In the same way, hearts and minds are protected by His peace, given by the Holy Spirit.

We must not allow anxieties or worries to break in and kill the peace. This is where we can practice the promise that "if we confess our sins to him, he can be depended on to forgive us and to cleanse us from every wrong. [And it is perfectly proper for God to do this for us because Christ died to wash away our sins]" (1 John 1:9).

"May the Lord of peace himself give you his peace no matter what happens" (2 Thess. 3:16).

V

Why do people keep saying lost?

While we were having dinner one night a family came to our door and said, "We are very sorry that you have lost your son." This word "lost" became a very common word to us for the next few months. What were people saying when they said we had lost our loved one? The way the word was being used it seemed to say a number of different things. The word seemed to imply "uncertain location" of the person, or that the person was not claimed. The most devastating thing was that he was no longer known, and this said that he no longer existed.

So the question came to us: Can something be lost when you know where it is? Never. It is impossible for someone to be lost when you know where he is. The apostle Paul knew that to be "absent from the body" was to be "present with the Lord." Therefore, when our loved ones sleep in death, they are with the Lord, not lost.

Our loved one has joined millions of others who have gone on before us to be with the Lord. His person is gone physically, but is very much alive in the presence of God.

It is also very true that our loved one's body will be brought to life and changed by God, so that we shall **all** be together someday with our wonderful Lord. "But the fact is that Christ did actually rise from the dead, and has become the first of millions who will come back to life again some day" (1 Cor. 15:20). Our loved one is enjoying a new life in the presence of the Lord.

Yes, we experience loneliness here in the absence of our loved one, but "it will all happen in a moment, in the twinkling of an eye, when the last trumpet is blown. For there will be a trumpet blast from the sky and all the Christians who have died will suddenly become alive with new bodies that will never, never die; and then we who are still alive shall suddenly have new bodies, too" (1 Cor. 15:52). That is just how quickly we shall all be united again, so that we can honestly say that our separation is only temporary, not permanent.

Nothing is lost when you know where it is—praise God!

"Why search among the dead for the one who lives?"

(Luke 24:5, NEB).

VI

Where is he?

This is a question that all loved ones are concerned about. "Where is he?" Once we stopped thinking about ourselves for a few moments, we started to think about our loved one. This question brought us back to the fact that life is more than just the physical and a person is more than just a body. Every person is an eternal being carried around for a few years in a physical body. God had breathed into man the breath of life and man became a living soul.

Man has a whole eternity either in the presence of God or out of the presence of God.

A person has free moral choice, and this is made on the acceptance of the finished work of Jesus Christ or the rejection of His work on behalf of the individual. Where is he? The believers are present with the Lord: that is the location of a loved one who is absent from the body. What a wonderful place to be—with the Lord Jesus Christ. The Bible declares that life with Him there is a great deal different from life on this old earth.

In heaven Mark Salisbury will still be Mark Salisbury. He must be himself, for he can be no other person. He has taken into heaven his personal identity, and he will retain it forever, for the Bible says: "And if anyone's name was not found recorded in the Book of Life, he was thrown into the Lake of Fire" (Rev. 20:15). There are real names written in the Book of Life, so that a person will be known by his name. Therefore, our son is the same person we knew here on earth.

It is true that someday we shall all receive new bodies, but we shall still be the same people. The individuality of each person is more real in heaven than here on earth. For our loved one is more truly himself today than when he inhabited his physical body. He could never be his best in the old body, but in heaven he is at his best.

He has gone to join millions of others who have said "yes" to God's love. Yes—our loved ones are with the Lord, and with Paul, Peter, and all believers who have lived down through the years.

In the most literal way, God has said to Mark: "You have come right up into Mount Zion, to the city of the living God, the heavenly Jerusalem, and to the gathering of countless happy angels; and to the church, composed of all those registered in heaven; and to God who is Judge of all; and to the spirits of the redeemed in heaven, already made perfect; and to Jesus himself..." (Heb. 12:22-24).

"In thy presence is the fullness of joy" (Ps. 16:11, NEB).

VII

Will he live again?

As we stood by that open grave with loved ones all around us, we took the last look at the casket. The great question at that moment was, "Will he live again?" This was a question that had to be answered if we were going to go on at all. We went back to the source book about God— the Bible. The Bible is "true-truth." But what does the Bible teach about this question, "Will he live again?"

The Bible teaches that there will be a resurrection of the body of every person, whether that person is a believer or an unbeliever. Paul wrote: "Death came into the world because of what one man (Adam) did, and it is because of what this other man (Christ) has done that now there is the resurrection from the dead" (1 Cor. 15:21). Every person will have a body because of the bodily resurrection of Jesus Christ.

Jesus Christ is risen from the dead. The major difference between Christianity and all of the religions of the world is in the historical fact that Christ's grave was empty. This means that the person of Jesus Christ defeated the great enemy—death—by himself. He defeated death through His resurrection to eternal life. The great enemy in life is death, but praise God —death is defeated.

But, lest we doubt this, we have many witnesses to the fact of Christ's resurrection. Jesus Christ in His supernatural body was seen by Peter and the other twelve disciples. Peter had gone to the tomb of Jesus because he believed that his Lord was dead. He arrived there with his friend John, looked into the tomb, but did not see a body— only the limp grave clothes. This convinced him that Jesus Christ was alive, and so from firsthand experience Peter knew that the body of Jesus Christ had been raised.

Thomas, one of Jesus' disciples, said that he would never believe that Jesus Christ was not dead if he did not see His body. Though the women reported to Thomas, as did Peter, he refused to believe that Jesus Christ had gotten up out of the grave. But when Thomas saw the Lord and Jesus invited him to reach in and touch Him, Thomas confessed, "My Lord and my God!"

Moreover, the Lord was seen bodily by over 500 Christian people, and by James and Paul. For Paul says, "Last of all, I saw him, too."

Every new day, along with the sunrise and the sunset, reminds one of the resurrection. As spring comes with new life in all the earth, this is just a reminder in the external world that there is coming a day when the graves will be opened and every believer will put on a supernatural body which is incapable of dying. When this happens, then at last this scripture will come true: "Death is swallowed up in victory" (1 Cor. 15:54).

The death of death is in the bodily resurrection of Jesus Christ. Yes, death still retains temporary power over our bodies, for it has just taken my son. But Jesus Christ has struck death itself with a fatal wound, and in God's time death will be abolished forever. My loved one, just like yours, will not stay in that grave. Out of the dust God will raise up a new body, a supernatural body, at last immune to decay.

"Why is it considered incredible among you that God should raise dead men to life?" (Acts 26:8, NEB).

VIII

What will he be like?

Another question which came to our minds was, "What will our loved one look like?" Will he be the same as he was on earth? Will he still be a boy? Will he be a grown man? Just what will his body look like?

As a sorrowing mother and father, these were some of our thoughts.

The only place to turn was to the Bible, because it is the Word of God. The Bible teaches that God will give to every believer a new body, which will be resurrected from the old. There will be drastic changes in the old body, but the new one will resemble the body which the person had in this life.

Our Lord set the example in His own body. His supernatural body is the same kind of body which Mark is going to have on the great day of resurrection.

The resurrected Jesus Christ had a real body. He was not invisible spirit, but inhabited a real body, which looked like the body He had before He died. Jesus said to His disciples, "Look at my hands! Look at my feet! You can see that it is I, myself! Touch me and make sure that I am not a ghost! For ghosts don't have bodies, as you see that I do!" (Luke 24:39). The disciples were still undecided about whether Jesus had a real body or not, so He ate broiled fish and bread. Jesus Christ did not eat the food to nourish His body, but to prove to the disciples that His was a true body.

Jesus' body was visible, for the disciples saw Him at the Lake of Galilee and recognized who He was from about 100 yards away. By this we know that He must have looked like He did before He died. The body looked familiar, for in it lived the same Jesus Christ.

Through Jesus' example, we know that the supernatural body is not subject to the limitations of the physical body. "That evening the disciples were meeting behind locked doors, in fear of the Jewish leaders, when suddenly Jesus was standing there among them!" (John 20:19). Jesus Christ came right through shut doors with His supernatural body.

The new body can also defy gravity. "During the forty days after his crucifixion he appeared to the apostles from time to time, actually alive [in human form], and proved to them in many ways that it was really he himself they were seeing. And on these occasions he talked to them about the Kingdom of God" (Acts 1:3). "It was not long afterwards that he rose into the sky and disappeared into a cloud, leaving them staring after him" (Acts 1:9). The Scripture teaches, "Then we who are still alive and remain on the earth will be caught up with them [Mark and all believers] in the clouds to meet the Lord in the air and remain with him forever" (1 Thess. 4:17).

Here, then, are some contrasts between our natural (physical) body and our supernatural (spiritual) body: The first is that our natural body is perishable and decays, while the supernatural body is immune to decay and will never die. This means that there will be no disease, no headaches, no tiredness or sickness, because superhuman bodies simply will not decay or break down.

Second, our earthly bodies live in dishonor and humiliation, but our supernatural bodies will be raised in honor and glory. Man, made in God's image, disobeyed God, and out of this disobedience came the dishonor and humiliation of his body. The supernatural body will be like the Lord's body on the Mount of Transfiguration: "Now they woke up and saw Jesus covered with brightness and glory, and the two men standing with him" (Luke 9:32).

Third, the weak natural body stands in contrast to the power-charged supernatural body. Like a flashlight battery, the earthly body gradually "runs down," losing strength until it is completely spent. The supernatural body will have perpetual power for the eternal activities that will accompany our life of enjoying God forever.

Finally, because of its weaknesses, the physical body also limits our experience with God. In his physical body, Moses was not allowed to see the face of God. "My face you cannot see," God told him, "for no mortal man may see me and live" (Ex. 33:20, NEB). But one of the promises to be realized in our spiritual bodies is that we will see Him "face to face" (1 Cor. 13:12).

We may be certain, then, that the new body will be wholly adapted to live in the new heaven and the new earth. This will be a perfect body—praise God!

There are going to be many, many changes, but the personal identity will be forever retained. The superhuman body will characterize people as they have always been; that is, as individuals. Each person will have a body just like Christ's own glorious body throughout eternity.

> *"Yes, dear friends, we are already God's children, right now, and we can't even imagine what it is going to be like later on. But we do know this, that when he comes we will be like him, as a result of seeing him as he really is"*
> (1 John 3:2).

IX

Where will we be?

There is another question which came into our minds in those early hours after our boy had gone to be with the Lord. What about heaven? The only place to look for some real answers about heaven was in the Bible, the only book which tells the "true-truth" about the great place called Heaven.

The word "heaven" occurs some 550 times in Scripture. Jesus Christ referred to heaven frequently, saying that He had come from heaven and that He was going to return to heaven. He said, "There are many homes up there where my Father lives, and I am going to perpare them for your coming. When everything is ready, then I will come and get you, so that you can always be with me where I am. If this weren't so, I would tell you plainly" (John 14:2, 3).

Jesus said that heaven is a real place, one that will provide a real home for all believers. He promised to prepare a real location, a place, for all saints. John says, in Revelation 21:3-4, "I heard a loud shout from the throne saying, 'Look, the home of God is now among men, and he will live with them and they will be His people; yes, God himself will be among them. He will wipe away all tears from their eyes, and there shall be no more death, nor sorrow, nor crying, nor pain. All of that has gone forever."

> HE WILL WIPE AWAY ALL TEARS FROM THEIR EYES, AND THERE SHALL BE NO MORE DEATH, NOR SORROW, NOR CRYING, NOR PAIN. ALL OF THAT HAS GONE FOREVER.

This is the kind of place heaven is and will always be. This is the place to which our loved one has gone. We call the great mystery "death," but angels call this "birth." It all depends upon one's perspective.

Mark can touch Christ from heaven's side, while we can through faith touch Him from earth's side. Therefore we can both meet in Him. Praise God!

Heaven is a place of eternal beauty, God's "showcase" of beauty in which He intends for His people to live. Heaven will be the place of rest, not the rest of doing nothing, but the perfect satisfaction of activity blessed of God. One activity will be intellectual, for there are many wonderful things to know and study about God. There we shall be able to comprehend much more and to learn much more quickly. "In the same way, we can see and understand only a little about God now, as if we were peering at his reflection in a poor mirror; but someday we are going to see him in his completeness, face to face. Now all that I know is hazy and blurred, but then I will see everything clearly, just as clearly as God sees into my heart right now" (1 Cor. 13:12).

Another heavenly pursuit will be social activity. Man was not created to live alone but to be with people and to have friends. Social life on earth, we know, is too often described as "impure thoughts; eagerness of lustful pleasure; idolatry, spiritism (that is, encouraging the activity of demons), hatred and fighting, jealousy and anger, constant effort to get the best for yourself, complaints and criticisms, the feeling that everyone else is wrong except those in your own little group, ... wrong doctrine, envy, murder, drunkenness, wild parties, and all that sort of thing. Let me tell you again as I have before, that anyone living that sort of life will not inherit the kingdom of God" (Gal. 5:19-21). But heaven's "social life" will take place on a different plane. Heaven is a wonderful place because of the things that **won't** be there as well as the people who **will** be there.

John saw heaven and said, "Nothing evil will be permitted in it—no one immoral or dishonest—but only those whose names are written in the Lamb's Book of Life" (Rev. 21:27). There will be no alienations in heaven, but there will be perfect people in a perfect environment, able to have perfect love and perfect communications. Praise God!

"Sometimes I want to live and at other times I don't, for I long to go and be with Christ. How much happier for ME than being here!"
(Phil. 1:23).

X

Can we go on?

This question, "Can we go on?" is always a big question in such an experience as this. The question is "for real," because loneliness is there when one misses the person who has gone home to God.

Loneliness is often a mood, but it can be more than that. It can be an all consuming feeling of being forsaken, abandoned, with the crushing conviction that one is all alone.

I remember the evening that Mark went to be with the Lord—our home was full of people, but it seemed empty. People talked, but their words did not reach me. I knew they meant well, but my soul was all alone. Only God could speak to me, and He did in the Bible: "But when the Father sends the Comforter instead of [to represent] me—and by the Comforter I mean the Holy Spirit—he will teach you much as well as remind you of everything I myself have told you" (John 14:26). The Holy Spirit of God came to me and said, "You are not alone, but I am with you. I am here to give you comfort—trust Me." "I am leaving you with a gift—peace of mind and heart! And the peace I give isn't fragile like the peace the world gives. So don't be troubled or afraid" (John 14:27). The greatest antidote for my loneliness has been the Scriptures, as taught to me by the Holy Spirit.

The question already asked in this small book always returns when I miss Mark: "Where is he?" The answer comes back with great joy: "He is with the Lord." I say to myself, "It would not be fair to ask Mark to come back after having been with the Lord." Yes, I am lonely for my son. But, praise God, I know where he is right now. My loneliness is answered by the purpose and program of God. God is going to work all of these things out—because He is God. David felt the same way at times, and his words are a comfort to meditate on: "The Lord is my shepherd, I shall not want. He maketh me to lie down in green pastures. He leadeth me beside still waters. He restoreth my soul: he leadeth me in paths of righteousness for his name's sake. Yea, though I walk through the valley of the shadow of death, I will fear no evil; for thou art with me; thy rod and Thy staff, they comfort me" (Ps. 23:1-4, KJV).

The answer to loneliness? It is the consciousness of the presence of the God who **is** there. The God who delivers me from loneliness at the deepest level of my being.

How can I be met at the deepest level of my sorrow? Because I know where Mark is. Our separation is only for a time, not forever. I know that we shall meet again, just as the Lord has said over and over again. I know that he is safe, and this satisfies my concern as a parent.

Sometimes I feel like the only person in the world who has had a loved one go to be with the Lord. But this is not so. Let me share an Eastern legend about a Hindu woman whose only child had died. She went to a prophet to ask for her child back. The prophet told her to go and obtain a handful of rice from a house into which death had not come. If she could obtain the rice in this way, he promised to give her the child back. From door to door she asked the question: "Are you all here around the table—father, mother, children—none missing?" But always the answer came back that there were empty chairs in each house. As she continued on, her grief and sorrow were softened as she found that death had visited all families. Yes, death is universal: our painful experience is not the only one of its kind. Because God is faithful, because Jesus Christ is alive, so is your loved one and mine.

Some people would say in our loneliness that we "lost" our loved one. Not true. Our loved ones are gone from us, but not lost. They are more alive today than the day before they died physically. We feel loneliness because we miss their physical presence, but they are alive and joyful in the presence of the Lord.

My wife and I still have two children, Mark and Janna. The only difference is that Mark now lives in heaven while Janna lives in our earthly home. All are still in the family of God—that has not been changed. Physical death has not altered the fact that

Mark is our son—he will always be our son. You still have that son or daughter or mother or dad who has died; physical death cannot eliminate that person. They have moved on to the home of all Christians.

The old song is right: "This world is not my home, I'm just a passing through." Our home is with our Father and God. "For this world is not our home; we are looking forward to our everlasting home in heaven" (Heb. 13:14). Some lives are shorter than others. It is not the **duration** of life that counts, but the **donation** of the life. Not quantity of life, but quality of life—that is the important thing. All of Mark's life was lived for God. What wonderful joy to be able to say that!

"I saw emptiness under the sun: a lonely man without a friend, without son or brother, toiling endlessly yet never satisfied with his wealth—'For whom,' he asks, 'am I toiling and denying myself the good things of life?'" (Eccles. 4:7, 8, NEB).

"The spirit of the Lord God is upon me because the Lord has anointed me . . . to bind up the brokenhearted" (Isa. 61:1, NEB).

XI

How can we fill the void?

Driving down the street past the basketball court where both of us had played basketball only a few days before leaves me with a great emptiness in my stomach. Knowing that we are not going to be playing basketball together, or talking together just leaves a great big void. Is there any hope for filling this void?

God gives hope in sorrow. "And now, dear brothers, I want you to know what happens to a Christian when he dies so that you will not be full of sorrow when it happens, like those are who have no hope" (1 Thess. 4:13). This is called the "blessed hope" of the Christian, because we know that our hope is in God, not in the world. This scripture gives us the reassurance that we are not like people who have no hope. Why do we have this hope? Because of the promised return of Jesus Christ. "For since we believe that Jesus died and then came back to life again, we can also believe that when Jesus returns, God will bring back with him all the Christians who have died" (1 Thess. 4:14).

> AND THE BELIEVERS WHO ARE DEAD WILL BE THE FIRST TO RISE TO MEET THE LORD.

Praise the Lord—Mark is coming back! Your loved one is coming back. Jesus Christ is coming back. God is going to bring all of the Christians back with Him—wonderful! What a great group of people that is going to be. "I can tell you this direct from the Lord: that we who are still living when the Lord returns will not rise to meet him ahead of those who are in their graves" (1 Thess. 4:15).

This is right from the Lord. The Scriptures are inspired by the Holy Spirit of God and constitute the infallible revelation of God to man. "For the Lord himself will come down from heaven with a mighty shout and with the soul-stirring cry of the archangel and the great trumpet-call of God. And the believers who are dead will be the first to rise to meet the Lord" (1 Thess. 4:16).

One Sunday morning, just two months before my son went to be with the Lord, I spoke on this section of Scripture. During the message Mark wrote down a number of questions to ask me after the message. One question was about this verse. "If people (Christians) die and their soul goes to heaven and their physical body stays in the grave, how can the soul in the Rapture go up and meet their heavenly body in the air if their soul is in heaven?" He was only 12 at the time. The answer is in the Bible. The spirit of man goes to be with the Lord, ". . . to be absent from the body, and to be present with the Lord" (2 Cor. 5:8).

The life of the spirit is independent of the physical body in which it resides. F. B. Meyer said, "Death is not a state, but an act; not a condition, but a passage." But out of what remains in the ground God will bring forth a supernatural body. This is resurrection, a wholly new issue of life springing from the "seed" that was planted. "Don't be so surprised! Indeed the time is coming when all the dead in their graves will hear the voice of God's Son, and shall rise again—those who have done good, to eternal life; and those who have continued in evil, to judgment" (John 5:28, 29).

Out of that grave will come a new superhuman body for Mark. His spirit will come down with the Lord, and at the same time a new superhuman body will go up to unite with it forever. The spirit is never complete without a body. What about the rest of us? "Then we who are still alive and remain on the earth will be caught up with them in the clouds to meet the Lord in the air and remain with him forever" (1 Thess. 4:17). This will be one of the greatest events in the history of the world: the reunion of all believers and their Lord.

One thinks of family reunions, but this will be the greatest—our family, your family will be united with our God. And this will be forever because we shall be in the land of the living. Our bodies will be immune to decay—immortality has overtaken us. "So comfort each other with this news" (1 Thess. 4:18). What great news? That someday you and I will leave the land of the dying to go to the land of the living with our loved ones.

"Encourage the fainthearted" (1 Thess. 5:14, NEB).

XII

What will the future be?

This is a question which is on the heart and mind of every person who goes through this experience. We asked ourselves, "What will the future be?" The only book which can really tell the future is the Bible.

One day as Jesus was leaving the temple grounds, His disciples wanted to take Him on a tour. But He told them, " 'All these buildings will be knocked down, with not one stone left on top of another!' 'When will this happen?' the disciples asked him later, as he sat on the slopes of the Mount of Olives. 'What events will signal your return, and the end of the world?'" (Matt. 24:2-3). There is no doubt on the part of Bible-believing people today that Jesus Christ is going to return. The question is, when?

The disciples wanted to know if there were signs preceding the Lord's return. Jesus Christ said that there would be signs preceding His coming. But He warned the disciples not to set dates: "But no one knows the date and hour when the end will be—not even the angels. No, nor even God's Son. Only the Father knows" (Matt. 24:36). But the fact is that Jesus Christ is coming back. Billy Graham said, "Today it would seem that those signs are indeed converging for the first time since Christ ascended into heaven."

There are many signs preceding the return of our Lord, but we know from our Bible that when the Lord returns, He will bring our loved ones with Him. Praise the Lord! So we sorrow not as people who have no hope. Our hope is in the return of Jesus Christ, the One who turns our sorrow into joy! Look up—He is coming on the clouds...

Yes, Jesus Christ is going to come back to this earth with all of His people and will rule over the earth as King of Kings and Lord of Lords. This will last for 1,000 years—with all of God's people being rulers. "They had come to life again and now they reigned with Christ for a thousand years" (Rev. 20:4). This shall be the time of unusual peace, prosperity, long life and the whole earth will be full of righteousness. "He shall be very great and shall be called the Son of God. And the Lord God shall give him the throne of his ancestor David. And he shall reign over Israel forever; his kingdom shall never end!" (Luke 1:32, 33).

Something of the great peace and beauty of these days is recorded in Isaiah 11: 6-10. The Lord shall rule from the City of Jerusalem "when the Lord of hosts shall reign in Mount Zion, and in Jerusalem, and before his ancients gloriously" (Isa. 24:23, Authorized).

Think of the great future God has for His children. The unbeliever is having his best days now, with the worst days ahead. But we Christians have only the greatest days ahead. The return of Jesus Christ is one of the great events in history, an event all Christians look forward to.

Just think of the time we all will have with our supernatural bodies living and ruling on the earth for the thousand years with Jesus Christ. Prevailing righteousness—praise God! Peace—praise God! We have a great God and a great future!

The conditions existing during the millennium will be poured out upon the earth through the Lord Jesus Christ. There will be a cessation of war, because all will be under the rule of Jesus Christ. National and individual peace will be the fruit of Christ's reign. Fullness of joy and holiness will be the portion of all. There will be perfect justice, perfect comfort, because the King will personally minister both of these to every individual. Full knowledge and instruction will come through the teaching ministry of the Holy Spirit. There will be abundant productivity on the earth, with the animals changed so as to lose their venom and ferocity. Sickness will be removed, along with fear of oppression—all a gift from the King. There will be a manifest presence of God and fullness of the Holy Spirit. This is the time all mankind has looked forward to down through the years.

    Don't think in terms of a "dim future" for that loved one who has gone to be with Christ. The future is bright! "For I know the plans I have for you, says the Lord, plans for welfare and not for evil, to give you a future and a hope" (Jer. 29:11, RSV).

> *"For Christ will be King until He has defeated all his enemies, including the last enemy—death. This too must be defeated and ended"* (1 Cor. 15:26).

XIII

What has been gained?

The question presses itself on us: "What has been gained through this experience?" The experience through which we have passed has been a painful one, but have we learned something? Yes, we have! The world is a classroom, not a playfield, as some people think.

I learned and am learning many things from the experience of having our teenaged son go to be with the Lord. "Jesus Christ is the same yesterday, today and forever" (Heb. 13:8). He is no different today than He was yesterday. The fact that our son is now with Him has not changed Jesus Christ. As always, He regains faithful and wonderful to me.

I learned anew and afresh the helplessness of man, the impossibility of comforting someone in deep sorrow, the futility of trying to stop something from happening. Though he may think otherwise, man does not sit at the controls of this old world. The non-Christians could only say "I am sorry." They could offer no hope to us as a family.

I learned in a deeper way what I had believed from the day I was born again—that the Bible is true-truth. God has spoken through propositional form the truth concerning himself, man, history, the universe. The Bible is the revelation of God himself to man.

I learned again that God has all knowledge, and that my part is to trust Him because He knows. I do not know all there is to know—God does.

God made Mark for purposes that could be finished on earth in 12 years. He knows—I trust.

I learned time after time that prayer does reach the heavenly ear. Communion with God is a wonderful experience. It involves my coming to God through the Lord Jesus Christ, a time of simply loving God, enjoying His presence, thinking about Him, adoring Him and thanking Him for all that He has done for me. There is a time of prayer when I ask God for help—when I need things.

I learned the true consolation that could come only from the fellow believers. Even as believers, we have our trials and problems, but on the deepest level it was only the Christian who could identify with us and offer hope. Many brought food, called, sent cards, mailed money, helped in our home. Christians are wonderfully different—praise God!

I learned that a compassionate pastor is a wonderful person to know during those days. Our pastor was a tremendous help during those first few days. His being right there, his guiding us through all the things that must be taken care of during those hours, was truly appreciated.

How wonderful God has been in answering our prayers. Then there has been the intercessory prayer of so many of God's people on our behalf. People have reached up for us, and God has poured peace into our souls in answer to the prayers of His saints.

I learned that heaven is a real and wonderful place, and that part of my life is already there. I am looking forward to that day when Jesus Christ comes back with, and for, His saints.

Yes, Mark is gone, but he is with our wonderful Lord.

I learned that the answer does not lie in trying to forget. Mark's death can't be dismissed. I cannot rid my life of this memory, because he was a part of my life—and always will be. His chair can be sat in, but never filled by another. There is no peace in forgetfulness.

I learned that ceaseless activity does not satisfy, nor does filling my life with people and noise. I could run madly from place to place, but this does not bring peace.

I learned that retreating from the world carries no peace. I tried avoiding people, speaking engagements, any gathering where people might ask about Mark or express their regret. But I found no peace in withdrawal—only more loneliness.

I learned that peace came through agreeing with God's will. This has not made death an easy path—but it released me from the tension of struggling against God in addition to my grief. The cross was neither pleasant nor easy for the Lord, but He said, "I will to do thy will, O my father; thy will, and not Mine, be done." Peace comes through resting our case with God, saying, "Your will be done, because your will is right."

We can comfort others only when we have been through the experience ourselves. I know this is true because of my own life. Before Mark introduced us to death, I did not have the sympathy nor the heartbeat to encourage others. I did not know how they felt. But now I know. I had never before faced death head-on. Now, through experience, I know the crushing weight of its seeming finality.

One of the best ways to express grief is through our tears. I do thank God for the release of tears that has been a great help to me. Jesus Christ wept at the tomb of His friend in the presence of adults. This God-given release needs to be used in honestly expressing our grief.

But for now there are some answers as to what we can do with this experience. Paul, in writing to his Christian friends in the city of Corinth, said, "What a wonderful God we have—he is the Father of our Lord Jesus Christ, the source of every mercy, and the one who so wonderfully comforts and strengthens us in our hardships and trials. And why does he do this? So that when others are troubled, needing our sympathy and encouragement, we can pass on to them this same help and comfort God has given us" (2 Cor. 1:3, 4).

We can take this experience and our faith in God (the only true hope) and comfort those who, like us, stand in great need. May God help you to share your victory in Him.

"Bend your necks to my yoke, and learn from me, for I am gentle and humble-hearted; and your souls will find relief" (Matt. 11:29, NEB).

MARK

You were everything
A little sister could want.
Although we had our differences,
We were great pals.
You helped me
Through all my problems
And that made life seem easier.
You were so special—
And still are.
I long for the day
When we shall see each other again.
I want to get to know you again
In only a way a sister can.
It is hard growing up without
    a brother,
But I want the best for you
And you are in the best
Right now.
I know you still love me
As much as I love you.
Thank you for still being
My brother.

Janna Salisbury
November 10, 1975